COLLINS GEM
CATS
a mine of information

COLLINS GEM
Chinese
ASTRO
a mine of information

D1759217

COLLINS GEM
HORSES
& PONIES
a mine of information

COLLINS GEM
INSECTS
a mine of information

COLLINS GEM
**KINGS &
QUEENS**
a mine of information

COLLINS GEM
MUSHROOMS
& TOADSTOOLS
a mine of information

COLLINS GEM
SNAKES
a mine of information

COLLINS GEM
SPIDERS
a mine of information

COLLINS GEM
STRESS
Survival Guide
a mine of information

COLLINS GEM
TAROT
a mine of information

COLLINS GEM
WINE
Guide
a mine of information

COLLINS GEM
WORLD
atlas
a mine of information

COLLINS GEM
YOGA
a mine of information

COLLINS GEM
ZODIAC
Types
a mine of information

HarperCollins Publishers
PO Box, Glasgow G4 0NB

First published 1999

Reprint 10 9 8 7 6 5 4 3 2 1 0

© The Foundry Creative Media Co. Ltd, 1999 (text)

ISBN 0 00 472311-2

All pictures courtesy of Topham except for: Foundry Arts: pp.
13(t), 66(t), 100(t); Pictorial Press: pp. 14(t), 185(t); London
Features: pp. 29(b); Popperfoto: pp. 42(b), 43(b), 68(b);
C.F.C.L./Image Select: pp. 76(t), 145(t); Image Select: pp. 159(t);
Christie's Images: pp. 35(b), 97(t); Allsport: pp. 90(t), 109(b),
124(t), 135(r), 135(b), 179(t); Allsport/Hulton Getty: pp. 101(b)

Created and produced by Flame Tree Publishing, part of
The Foundry Creative Media Co. Ltd
Crabtree Hall, Crabtree Lane, Fulham, London SW6 6TY

Thank you to the film companies, record companies and TV
companies who allowed usage of record covers/production stills.
Every effort has been made to contact copyright holders. In the
event of an oversight, the publishers will be pleased to rectify any
omissions in future editions of this book.

With special thanks to Josephine Cutts, Claire Dashwood,
Helen Johnson, Dave Jones and Helen Tovey

Printed in Italy by Amadeus S.p.A.

COLLINS GEM

1970s

**Nigel Gross Graeme Kay
Damian Wild Sue Wood**

HarperCollins*Publishers*

Contents

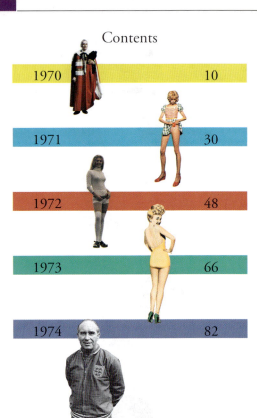

1975   100

1976   117

1977   134

1978   152

1979   168

How To Use This Book

This book covers a wide spectrum of the events that helped to define the 1970s: events of world prominence – Rhodesia gaining independence, India's first atomic bomb test, the Birmingham pub bombing, Watergate – alongside those of a less portentous nature – Sir John Betjeman becoming Poet Laureate, Red Rum winning the Grand National, the invention of Gillette's first safety razor. Sports, fashion, popular culture, science, the environment, literature, fine art, world news, cinema, theatre and music are all included. Events as diverse as Charlie Chaplin's knighthood and Margaret Thatcher becoming the UK's first female Prime Minister; the kidnapping of Patty Hearst and the opening of *The Life of Brian*. Important births, deaths and marriages are included, as are book publications, record releases, first nights and film premieres.

1970s is divided in two ways: the contents page lists the page number at which each year of the decade begins, and every year is divided into individual months. Some months are contained on one page and some cover two pages. People, events and inventions all feature within each month, providing a comprehensive look at the true spirit of the age. Every month also features a variety of entry length: some simply a few words, some of several lines. In order to preserve the balance of *Zeitgeist*, every theme is afforded prominence in rotation throughout the book. As a result, not every major entry refers necessarily to an event of international significance; instead it may refer to an important fashion trend, an exciting sporting moment or the death of a leading artist.

A comprehensive index at the end of the book assists readers who wish to look up specific entries or subjects, but are unsure of the month or year in which they occurred.

A The page number appears in a colour-coded box that indicates which year you are looking at.

B Each month is indicated at the head of the appropriate page. Some months appear on one page, some over two depending on the number of relevant entries.

C The date of the event appears at the start of the entry. Entries with no date, but which are known to have happened in the specified month, appear at the top of the list.

D Entries differ in length from a few words to several lines.

E Every page is illustrated with topical photographs or drawings.

F Tint boxes indicate events that happened in the year, but not necessarily the month, in which they feature.

Icons represent the following themes:		
		Music
	science and technology	political events
	human interest	sporting events

Introduction

The 1970s was an era of diversity and change. It saw the UK join the Common Market; the US shocked by the scandal of Watergate; the investigation of Jupiter and Mars; and Argentina and Britain experience their first female Prime Ministers. Countries gained independence, economies nose-dived through recession and Everest was conquered by a female climber. Alongside all this, disco arrived, punk hit the streets and Bay City Rollermania sent teenage hormones through the roof.

After the Space Race of the 1960s, the field of science continued to thrive as governments craved more and more information. The 1970s also saw a spectacular array of domestic and humane inventions: from the Rubik's cube and the Sony Walkman to the first nuclear-powered pacemaker and the bionic arm. The Computer Age was finally accessible and the

motor industry began to build magnificent production cars; conversely environmental awareness also expanded – Greenpeace guarded the seas and those in power started to examine solar power and the effects of CFCs.

Overall it was an exciting decade during which the Vietnam War at last came to an end. An era in which music divided, mutated and exploded into several new genres; fashion re-created itself, adding disco and punk to its repertoire; and the women's liberation and gay rights movements really took off. The decade can be experienced through the art and literature of the time: from Bob Dylan's *Blood on the Tracks* to William Walton's *2nd Bagatelle for Guitar*; the film of *Grease* to *Last Tango in Paris*; and Solzhenitsyn's *The Gulag Archipelago* to *Oz* magazine.

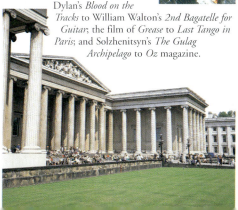

1970

January 1970

Rolf Harris tops the UK charts with 'Two Little Boys'.

Germaine Greer's feminist tract *The Female Eunuch* is published in the UK. Australian-born Greer has rocked the literary world with her intelligently written, thought-provoking exposé of female stereotyping. The book is set to change the way the world looks at feminist writing forever.

Feminist Germaine Greer

1st The UK government scraps the ruling that a maximum of £50 is allowed to be taken abroad. This decision (which came into effect in 1967) gave an enormous boost to the package-holiday industry.

Australian-born entertainer, Rolf Harris

2nd The meteoric career of Manchester United's talented footballer, George Best, hits a rocky patch. The Northern Ireland international is suspended by the Football Association for a month, after being found guilty of 'bringing the game into disrepute'.

13th The African breakaway state of Biafra surrenders and is retaken by Nigeria.

16th British deaths from Hong Kong flu are rising, with 2,850 recorded in the first week of the year.

21st First scheduled flight of the Jumbo Jet.

Moscow waitresses wearing masks as protection against flu

February 1970

2nd Bertrand Russell dies.

2nd Joe Frazier knocks out Jimmy Ellis in New York to take the world heavyweight title.

2nd The first successful human nerve transplant is carried out in Munich, Germany.

3rd In London, the police close The Open Space Theatre, after a private showing of the sex movie *Flesh* provokes complaints of obscenity. *Flesh* was produced by Andy Warhol and directed by Paul Morrissey. The secretary of the BBFC (British Board of Film Categorisation) denies the accusations.

Film producer and artist Andy Warhol

11th The UK's National Health Service is to establish 90 health authorities to oversee individual regions.

20th Timothy Leary, candidate for the California governorship and advocate of LSD, is sentenced to 10 years in jail for possession of marijuana.

A smiling Dr Timothy Leary leaving court

21st Simon and Garfunkel's *Bridge Over Troubled Water* enters the UK charts.

23rd Rolls Royce have requested £50 million in Government aid to help fund the new RB211 jet engine.

March 1970

1st You can now dial direct between London and New York without needing the operator.

2nd The UK's rebel African colony, Rhodesia, which illegally proclaimed independence under white control in 1965, becomes a republic.

8th Oxford sees the premiere of Samuel Beckett's one-minute play *Breath*.

12th The UK Government has extended its quarantine on animals entering the country; it will now be a full year. The move is primarily aimed at preventing the deadly disease rabies from entering the country.

RABIES IS A KILLER

Rabies is a horrifying and very painful disease which affects both animals and human beings. There is no known cure.

Rabies is widespread in Europe and is a serious threat to Britain. One infected animal could bring it permanently into this country. Quarantine is an essential safeguard against rabies

Smuggling of animals including pets can be punished by unlimited fines and up to a years imprisonment.

Illegally imported animals may also be destroyed.

KEEP RABIES OUT OF BRITAIN

International direct dialling is available on all telephones

Newly-weds. David and Angie Bowie

20th David Bowie marries Mary Angela Barnetty at Bromley Registry Office.

23rd 18 Thalidomide victims have been awarded a total of £369,409 in compensation. Thalidomide, a tranquiliser given to pregnant women, caused many severe birth defects.

Open University starts in the UK.

24th Henry Cooper defeats Jack Bodell to regain the British heavyweight boxing crown. He first won the title in 1959.

April 1970

10th **A new 'get tough' policy** is adopted in Northern Ireland as British troop reinforcements fly in.

15th **Canon produces an electronic calculator** small enough to be carried in a pocket.

17th *Apollo 13* **returns safely to Earth** at last, nearly four days after an explosion. The module containing the vessel's oxygen and water had been severely damaged but the Lunar Module was undamaged. This provided the crew with a safe area until the ship could land.

Golfer Tony Jacklin wins the US Open – he is the first Briton to do so since 1920.

18th Production of the Morris **Minor**, the UK's longest-running car, finally comes to an end. The first Minor appeared in 1948.

21st Bernice Rubens wins the Booker Prize for her novel *The Elected Member*.

27th US actor Tony Curtis is fined £50 for possession of cannabis in the UK.

Apollo 13

30th President Richard Nixon orders US troop attacks on Communist strongholds in neutral Cambodia.

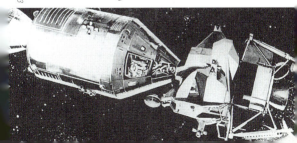

May 1970

4th **Members of the US's National Guard** fire into a crowd of unarmed student demonstrators at Kent State University, Ohio, as an anti-war protest turns violent, killing four and wounding 11. The demonstration was triggered by fresh US involvement in Cambodia.

26th **England football captain Bobby Moore** is accused of stealing a bracelet in Bogota, Colombia. Later it is discovered he was set-up by the shop's owners.

28th **Setsuko Watanabe reaches an altitude of 7,950 m** (26,223 feet) on Mount Everest – the highest so far by a woman.

Unarmed students clash with the National Guard

English football captain, Bobby Moore

June 1970

8th Author E. M. Forster dies. His novels include *A Room With A View* and *Howard's End*.

15th In the Queen's Birthday Honours List, Sir Laurence Olivier is given a life peerage for his 'services to the theatre'. Olivier, currently playing Shylock in *The Merchant of Venice*, is the first actor to be ennobled.

17th Rover announces its new model, the four-wheel-drive Range Rover.

26th Mid-Ulster MP Bernadette Devlin, 23, starts a six-month jail sentence for incitement to riot.

Lord Laurence Olivier

Impassioned public speaker, Bernadette Devlin

July 1970

Mungo Jerry's 'In The Summertime' reaches UK number 1.

7th Sir Allan Lane, creator of the Penguin paperback, dies.

12th Golfer Jack Nicklaus wins the British Open – his first major title for three years – at St Andrews.

15th In a London hospital, the first heart pacemaker powered by a nuclear battery has been surgically implanted in a human being.

16th The UK stands poised on the brink of a state of emergency as dockers stop work after their negotiations for pay increases breakdown. Troops may be called in to take over in an effort to keep ports running.

Doctors examine an experimental pacemaker

18th *Oh! Calcutta!*, Kenneth Tynan's controversial sex show, opens at the Round House in London.

21st The construction of Aswan High Dam, on the Nile in Egypt finishes – 10 years after the foundation stone was laid. In order to accommodate the Dam, the ancient temple of Abu Simbel was moved from its original site. The Dam's construction also led to extensive re-routing of the River Nile.

Oh! Calcutta!'s cast celebrate their first performance

Spectacular view from the Aswan Dam

August 1970

2nd In Northern Ireland, the British army are ordered to use rubber bullets.

12th The leaders of West Germany and the USSR sign a peace pact in Moscow. The two countries have been at odds since the Second World War. Soviet support for Communist East Germany has fuelled the disharmony.

13th A cache of IRA weapons has been found in Tooting, South-West London.

British troops patrol Belfast's streets

Windscale atomic complex, Cumbria

24th In the UK, part of the Windscale nuclear plant (now called Sellafield) has been shut after a radiation leak.

26th The second Isle of Wight pop festival begins, featuring a performance by Jimi Hendrix. Miles Davis, Leonard Cohen and The Doors all appear. Before it is over the promoters say there will not be a third festival because of rising losses.

31st In the US Deep South, a new school life dawns for thousands of pupils – this is the first day of desegregated schooling.

31st After 14 years the UK's National Youth Theatre gets a permanent home at the Shaw Theatre.

Brazil's footballers take the World Cup for the third time.

Isle of Wight crowds soak up the atmosphere

Rehearsals at the National Youth Theatre

September 1970

The first in-car cassette player goes on sale in the UK.

4th Following in the footsteps of Rudolph Nureyev, Russian ballerina Natalia Makarova (in the UK with the Kirov Ballet) applies for, and is granted, permission to stay in England.

Natalia Makarova defects from Russia

5th Austrian racing driver Jochen Rindt dies while practising before the Italian Grand Prix. Posthumously, he becomes the World Champion.

12th Concord makes its first landing at Heathrow amidst complaints about the noise.

12th In Jordan, Palestinian terrorists hold 56 people hostage after blowing up three hijacked airliners bound for the US.

Jochen Rindt

18th Less than a month after his Isle of Wight performance, Jimi Hendrix dies of a drug overdose in London.

London crowds mourn Nasser's death

28th Colonel Nasser, **President of Egypt** for 14 years, dies from a heart attack.

The Beatles, the world's most famous pop group of all time, split up.

IBM develop the 'floppy' disk for storing computer data.

October 1970

Liquid Crystal Displays (LCDs) are developed that are small enough to be used in electronic equipment.

At a mass Moonie wedding ceremony in Seoul, South Korea, 790 couples from all round the world are married by the leader of the controversial church, Sun Myung Moon.

1st The racehorse Nijinksy, winner of the Derby, 2000 Guineas and St Leger, loses to Sassafras in France's Arc de Triomphe race.

4th US singer Janis Joplin dies of a drug overdose in a Hollywood Hotel.

Nijinsky winning the Derby, June 1970

The emotive Janis Joplin

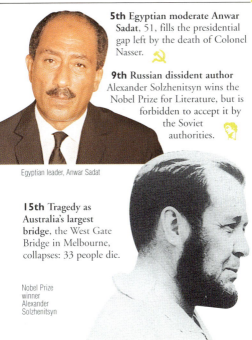

5th Egyptian moderate Anwar Sadat, 51, fills the presidential gap left by the death of Colonel Nasser.

9th Russian dissident author Alexander Solzhenitsyn wins the Nobel Prize for Literature, but is forbidden to accept it by the Soviet authorities.

Egyptian leader, Anwar Sadat

15th Tragedy as Australia's largest bridge, the West Gate Bridge in Melbourne, collapses: 33 people die.

Nobel Prize winner Alexander Solzhenitsyn

The New English Bible is published this year.

November 1970

6th NASA launches a military 'Spy' satellite into orbit, claiming it can detect a missile launched from anywhere in the world. The Soviets protest vociferously.

10th In London, **Henry Cooper** regains his European heavyweight boxing title by defeating José Manual Ibar.

12th Former French president, **de Gaulle**, dies just days before his 80th birthday. Cinemas close throughout the country as the nation goes into mourning.

27th A new **homosexual organisation**, the Gay Liberation Front, holds its first UK public demonstration in London.

The congregation awaits the arrival of de Gaulle's coffin

Henry Cooper with manager, Jim Wicks

December 1970

Intel announces the introduction of the 1-kilobyte RAM chip, an enormous leap in capabilities for computers.

2nd MPs reject a call to keep British Summer Time going through winter.

20th Hundreds are reported **dead** as violence erupts across Poland in protest at rising food prices. Many were shot by militia. The raging week-long demonstrations against the government began in the port of Gdansk and rapidly spread to other towns.

George Harrison with his wife, Patti Boyd

26th George Harrison's 'My Sweet Lord', produced by Phil Spector, hits number 1 in the US.

1971

January 1971

2nd In Glasgow, 66 die in a crush at the Ibrox Park stadium, during a Rangers v. Celtic football match.

10th French fashion designer Coco Chanel dies, aged 87, in Paris. Her famous No.5 perfume was named after her lucky number; her suits were synonymous

The funeral of the fashion queen Gabrielle Coco Chanel

with French chic and she was partly responsible for the popularity of fashions as diverse as bobbed hair, suntans and costume jewellery.

22nd Shostakovich's ballet *The Dreamers*, based on his operas 22 and 27, premieres in Moscow.

Russia's great composer, Shostakovich

Murderer Charles Manson and his 'family'

25th Drug-crazed commune and cult leader **Charles Manson** is convicted by a Los Angeles court, together with three hippie followers. They are found guilty of horrifically killing the eight-months-pregnant actress, Sharon Tate, and six friends, in a frenzied attack at her luxury Beverley Hills home.

 25th The Ugandan president, **Milton Obote**, is ousted by army commander Idi Amin, who promises free elections and civilian rule.

Idi Amin, Uganda's new president

February 1971

4th It seems the end of an era for UK manufacturing as Rolls Royce declares itself bankrupt. The government later takes over.

5th *Apollo 14* lands safely on the Moon. It is the third manned vehicle to do so.

7th A referendum in Switzerland finally gives women the vote.

12th Patti Smith makes her stage debut, as a poet, at St Mark's Church, New York.

American singer, Patti Smith

Apollo crew: Stuart Roosa, Alan Sheppard, Edgar Mitchell

15th After years of debate, decimal currency is introduced in the UK: 12 pennies in a shilling and 20 shillings in £1 is replaced by 100 pence in £1. The florin is replaced by 10p and the threepenny bit, sixpence and half-crown cease.

17th After two months in Paris, the travelling Andy Warhol retrospective exhibition, including his screen-prints and other New Realist works, moves to the Tate Gallery in London for a six-week stay.

17th In Melbourne, England beat the Australians to regain the Ashes after 12 years.

Arsenal win the 1971 League and FA Cup Double.

March 1971

6th The UK sees its biggest-ever women's liberation demo with 4,000 women marching from Hyde Park to Downing Street in London. The demonstration's four main themes are equal pay, equal access to

Women campaign for freedom of choice over abortions

education, free abortion and contraception on demand, and adequate day-care and nursery provision.

7th Poet and novelist **Stevie Smith**, whose works include *Novel on Yellow Paper*, dies aged 68.

Author and poet, Stevie Smith

WILLS'S CIGARETTES.

HAROLD LLOYD.

8th US actor and comedian Harold Lloyd dies aged 77.

16th Simon and Garfunkel sweep the Grammy Awards with six trophies, including the double of Best Album and Best Song of the year.

16th Henry Cooper retires after losing his British, European and Commonwealth titles to Joe Bugner.

29th The government announces plans for 60 commercial radio stations covering the UK.

29th William Calley, a US Lieutenant, is convicted by court martial of murdering 20 Vietnamese civilians in the My Lai massacre.

April 1971

Bangladesh, formerly East Pakistan, declares itself independent.

Hot pants are the latest fashion, following on from the huge success of the miniskirt.

6th Igor Stravinsky, the Russian composer whose works include *The Rite of Spring*, dies in New York aged 88. Stravinsky, who studied under Rimsky-Korsakov, also composed for Diaghilev's controversial Ballets Russes.

19th The total of UK jobless reaches its highest level for over 30 years at 814,819.

22nd Jean-Claude 'Baby Doc' Duvalier becomes President of Haiti after Papa Doc dies.

President of Haiti, Jean Claude Duvalier

May 1971

London Bridge is taken, stone by stone, to the US and reassembled at Lake Havasu, Arizona. The luckless buyer erroneously believed he had bought Tower Bridge.

16th An attempt by senior government rebels to overthrow Egyptian President Anwar Sadat fails.

23rd Jackie Stewart moves closer to the world championship by winning the Monaco Grand Prix.

27th Joseph Losey's *The Go-Between* takes the Grand Prix at the 25th Cannes Film Festival.

London Bridge, being carefully loaded into boats

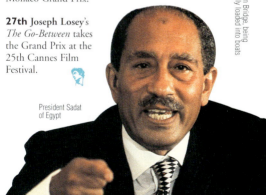

President Sadat of Egypt

June 1971

11th Playwright **Terence Rattigan**, whose works include *The Winslow Boy*, is awarded a knighthood in the Queen's Birthday Honours List.

15th Education Secretary Margaret Thatcher announces a controversial plan to scrap free school milk.

16th Baron Reith, the British broadcasting pioneer and former director-general of the BBC, dies aged 82.

Margaret Thatcher

17th Hewlett Packard **have installed a coin-operated computer** in a US library. It costs 15 cents for 2½ minutes.

The celebrated playwright, Terence Rattigan

19th *Opportunity Knocks* is the UK's most popular television show; it is watched by 6.6 million people.

28th In the US, the Supreme Court clears boxer Muhammad Ali of draft dodging.

30th The Soviet *Soyuz 11* spacecraft landed today. When ground crew reached the vehicles they found all three crew members dead. It would appear that the ship depressurised on re-entry,  though the reason for this remains unknown.

The first women priests are ordained in Hong Kong.

July 1971

2nd At Wimbledon, Australian teenager **Evonne Goolagong** beats Margaret Court to take the Women's Singles title.

3rd Doors singer **Jim Morrison dies** of heart failure at home in Paris. Self-styled rock poet, Morrison co-wrote classics like 'Light My Fire' and 'LA Woman'. He often found himself in trouble with the police for his outrageous stage antics.

The environmental pressure group, Greenpeace, is founded.

Louis Armstrong's Funeral

6th US singer and trumpeter Louis Armstrong dies.

6th A new law is passed in the UK: riders of motorcycles must wear crash helmets.

25th The world's first heart and lung transplant has been carried out in South Africa by Dr Christiaan Barnard.

26th Topless sunbathers on the French Riviera catch the eye of patrolling riot police who order them to cover up.

31st *Apollo 15* lands on the Moon carrying the Lunar Roving vehicle – or 'Moon buggy' – which astronauts drive on the Moon.

August 1971

1st **Sonny and Cher's** *Comedy Hour* is launched on CBS television in the US.

1st **The George Harrison-organised Concert for Bangladesh** takes place in New York's Madison Square Garden. Eric Clapton, Ravi Shankar and others play to a 40,000-strong crowd. Many thousands of Bangladeshis, decimated by the Pakistan army who are killing indiscriminately, now face starvation, disease and malnutrition after fleeing into India.

Singers, actors and presenters, Sonny and Cher

George Harrison and Ravi Shankar

The OZ editors are released on bail

5th The three editors of *OZ* magazine are imprisoned for publishing 'an obscene article'. The charge was brought against Jim Anderson, Richard Neville and Felix Dennis in 1970, after police seized copies of *OZ 28* (known as 'the School Kids' Issue').

6th Chay Blyth completes the first solo circumnavigation of the globe in a westerly direction.

11th The British Army and police, acting under emergency powers, seize 300 IRA suspects, for internment without trial, in Ulster. Major unrest follows.

11th UK Prime Minister Edward Heath wins the Admiral's Cup in his yacht *Morning Cloud*.

13th US space probe *Mariner 9* goes into orbit around Mars.

Chay Blyth being congratulated by Prince Philip

September 1971

5th Princess Anne, on Doublet, wins the European Three Day Event championship at Burghley Horse Trials.

6th Trouble-torn Ulster claims its 100th victim: a 14-year-old girl caught in Army-IRA crossfire.

11th Deposed Soviet leader Nikita Khrushchev, Russian ruler for eight years, dies a forgotten man.

29th In the second round of the European Cup Winners' Cup at Stamford Bridge, Chelsea beat Jeunnesse Hautcharage 13-0. This, added to the 8–0 lead from the first leg of the tie, adds up to a European aggregate record score of 21-0.

Princess Anne and Doublet

Mrs Nikita Khrushchev with her late husband

October 1971

Rock 'n' Roll deaths: Gene Vincent (12th); Duane Allman (29th).

9th The official visit to London by the Japanese Emperor, Hirohito, prompts a peaceful protest. Thousands line the roads to watch his procession to Buckingham Palace for a meeting with the Queen and Prince Philip. They display their public disapproval at his presence by preserving almost total quiet.

Emperor Hirohito, Empress Nakako and family

12th First performance of *Jesus Christ, Superstar* in New York.

26th In Argentina, eccentric American Bobby Fisher beats Tigran Petrosian in the world chess championships.

Chess champion
Bobby Fisher

November 1971

Micro skirts look set to take over from mini-skirts and hot pants as the latest style.

Intel announces the introduction of its new microchip – the 4004.

7th Two off-duty soldiers are murdered by the IRA in County Armagh. These are seen as tit-for-tat killings in the wake of last month's shooting by British soldiers of five people, two of them sisters, on the streets of Ulster.

12th The US *Mariner 9* starts to transmit photos of Mars.

13th Slade are UK number 1 with 'Coz I Love You'.

Top of the pops, Slade

December 1971

The British Royal family in the early 1970s

2nd The Queen gets a huge surprise pay rise, doubling her annual allowance to just under £1 million.

10th Frank Zappa is pushed off the stage at The Rainbow in London, fracturing his skull and breaking his leg.

17th India wins a two-week war against Pakistan after the defeated president, Yahya Khan, accepts a cease-fire.

20th London premiere of Stanley Kubrick's controversial film *A Clockwork Orange*. Adapted from Anthony Burgess's book, the futuristic story revolves around the violence-addicted character of Alex, played by Malcolm MacDowell.

A scene from *A Clockwork Orange*

1972

January 1972

1st French actor and singer **Maurice Chevalier**, star of the musical *Gigi*, dies aged 83.

9th Start of a **national coal strike** in the UK – in the heart of winter.

20th The **New York Stock Exchange** has its first female boss, Juanita Kreps.

Maurice Chevalier celebrating his 83rd birthday

The 1996 European flag flies alongside the Union Jack

22nd The UK finally joins the **Common Market** along with Ireland, Denmark and Norway.

25th The world's first **kidney and pancreas transplant** has been carried out in London.

25th The re-unification of Ireland is proposed by British MP Harold Wilson, leader of the Opposition. His plan would take effect in 1987.

30th Bloody Sunday: British troops open fire on civil-rights marchers in Londonderry, Northern Ireland. 13 die and 17 are wounded. Some MPs accuse the troops of mass murder, however the army chief defends his paratroopers, claiming they were shot at first.

Funeral of Bloody Sunday victims

February 1972

US President Richard Nixon

2nd The British Embassy in Dublin is burnt down by protesters, following the events of Bloody Sunday.

11th William Walton's *2nd Bagatelle for Guitar*, featuring Julian Bream, premieres at London's Queen Elizabeth Hall.

16th Cuts in power and the working week cripple a strike-hit Britain. The effects of the miners' pay dispute are felt throughout the country as industry limps along on a three-day week and nine-hour electricity blackouts bring the UK to a halt.

Miners' wives march in support of strike

A Living Wage

17th The 15,007,034th Volkswagen Beetle rolls off the production line, surpassing the record set by the Model T Ford.

The Volkswagen Beetle

19th America's 'A Horse with No Name' enters the US charts.

22nd US President Nixon visits Peking, re-establishing US links with the People's Republic of China.

27th South Lebanon is attacked by Israel in a tit-for-tat assault.

Tanks join the fight in Lebanon

Family TV show *The Waltons* starts in the US.

March 1972

2nd The US space probe *Pioneer 10* is launched towards Jupiter.

2nd 20 days of **power cuts** have come to an end in the UK as the miners' strike is settled.

Life continues by candlelight as strikes continue

3rd With a new stage name, after a string of earlier unsuccessful singles, Gary Glitter releases *Rock and Roll Parts 1&2*.

10th Walter Dejaco, who designed gas chambers in the Nazi death camp Auschwitz, is freed by a Viennese court.

British pop star, Gary Glitter

13th In New **York**, author Clifford Irving admits his 'autobiography' of Howard Hughes is a fake.

Clifford Irving, author of the Hughes biography hoax

18th T. Rex appear at **Wembley** as Bolanmania sweeps the UK. 20,000 people attend over the two nights: the band's first concerts for six months. Ringo Starr attends, intending to make a documentary on the event, and Bolan tells journalists he now has difficulty going out.

T. Rex on stage

20th *Apollo 16*, the fifth *Apollo* to land on the Moon, has touched down safely.

25th Edward Heath imposes direct rule from London for Northern Ireland.

29th William Walton's birthday is marked by premiere performances of *1st* and *3rd Bagatelle for Guitar*.

April 1972

10th The UN organises three separate ceremonies – London, Moscow and Washington – at which a treaty is signed to prohibit stocks of biological weapons. In total, 70 nations sign the treaty.

10th An earthquake in Iran kills an estimated 5,000 people. It measures 6.9 on the Richter scale.

10th William Friedkin's *The French Connection* wins 3 Oscars, including Best Film and Director.

16th Japanese novelist, Yasunari Kawabata, the first Japanese recipient of the Nobel Prize for Literature, commits suicide.

A scene from *The French Connection*

The first home-video recorders go on sale in the UK.

The musical *Grease* is first performed in New York.

22nd John Fairfax and his girlfriend Sylvia Cook are the first known people to cross the Pacific Ocean in a rowing boat. Their incredible voyage took them almost a year (361 days). They set off from San Francisco and finished at Hayman Island, Australia.

27th Five male-only Oxford University colleges are to admit women students.

The American flag flies in St Petersburg, to celebrate the signing of the biological weapons treaty

Magdelen College, one of Oxford's co-educational colleges

May 1972

John Edgar Hoover, the founder of the FBI and its director for nearly five decades, dies aged 77.

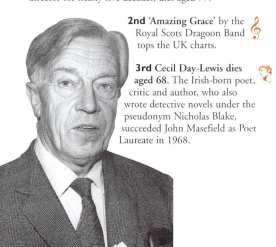

2nd 'Amazing Grace' by the Royal Scots Dragoon Band tops the UK charts.

3rd **Cecil Day-Lewis dies aged 68.** The Irish-born poet, critic and author, who also wrote detective novels under the pseudonym Nicholas Blake, succeeded John Masefield as Poet Laureate in 1968.

10th Slade begin their first major UK tour with Status Quo supporting.

22nd British actress Dame Margaret Rutherford, star of *Blithe Spirit* and a string of Agatha Christie films, dies.

24th Glasgow Rangers FC defeat the Moscow Dynamos 3–2 to win the European Cup Winners' Cup in Barcelona.

29th Nixon and Brezhnev sign the Moscow Pact, intended to reduce the risk of nuclear war.

Nixon visits Soviet leaders at the Kremlin

Alice Cooper hits number 1 with the single 'School's Out'.

The last *Goon Show* is broadcast.

June 1972

5th Following his death on 28 May, the Duke of
Windsor, who renounced the throne for love in 1936, is
returned to England to be buried. The Duchess attends
the funeral wearing a thick black veil. She sits with the
Queen and Prince Philip.

8th US blues singer **Jimmy Rushing**, one-time vocalist
with Count Basie, dies.

9th David Bowie releases his new LP,
The Rise and Fall of Ziggy Stardust.

17th The Watergate burglary takes
place.

18th An airliner crashes in a field just
after take-off from Heathrow, killing all
118 people on board.

Jimmy Rushing arriving for the Newport Jazz Festival

Dancing on the tables in *Hair*

July 1972

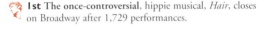

1st The **once-controversial**, hippie musical, *Hair*, closes on Broadway after 1,729 performances.

3rd The **first local TV station** has been granted for Plumstead Cable Vision in South-East London.

8th The **Wimbledon tennis tournament** is won by Stan Smith and Evonne Goolagong in the Singles finals. The tournament is suffering from the withdrawal of top-name players due to a dispute between World Championship Tennis and the International Lawn Tennis Association.

17th Bobby Fisher beats Boris Spassky in a controversial world chess championship match in Reykjavik.

August 1972

6th Idi Amin is expected to expel 50,000 Kenyan Asians within three months.

12th The ground war in Vietnam ends for the US with the withdrawal of the last US troops. Peace negotiations are under way in Paris. However, the war still continues from the air.

'Search and Destroy' mission by US marines

17th In an unprecedented legal move, all those involved in Gerard Damanio's soft-porn film, *Deep Throat*, are charged under a law preventing the transportation of obscene material over US state lines.

31st American swimmer Mark Spitz wins five gold medals at the Munich Olympic Games.

September 1972

🎼 Rod Stewart's 'You Wear It Well' reaches number 1.

5th 11 Israeli athletes die in an Arab terrorist attack at the Munich Olympics.

11th The television quiz show *MasterMind* begins broadcasting on the BBC.

15th The trial of those accused of breaking into the US Democratic party's Watergate headquarters begins in Washington. Two former White House aides, Howard Hunt and Gordon Liddy, are among seven men indicted.

The Senate investigation on Watergate

Armed police stand guard at the Olympics

October 1972

10th Sir John Betjeman **succeeds** the late Cecil Day-Lewis as Poet Laureate.

Poet Laureate, Sir John Betjeman

22nd Tragedy strikes England goalkeeper Gordon Banks as he loses an eye in a car crash.

26th Igor Sikorsky **dies** aged 83. Sikorsky was the pioneering inventor of the modern helicopter. Whilst many others had dabbled with the concept, it was Sikorsky who finally produced a working prototype in the 1930s.

Gordon Banks shouts advice to team mates

November 1972

The future of video games

'Tele-Tennis', the world's first video game, is installed in a Californian bar.

9th A human skull, found near Lake Rudolf in Kenya and believed to be nearly 2.5 million years old, is exhibited in London. Top archaeologists have painstakingly pieced all the bone fragments back together to form a complete skull.

26th The UK sees the new Race Relations Act implemented. This aims to wipe out racial discrimination in the workplace.

Racial discrimination at work is made illegal in the UK

December 1972

Anti-obscenity campaigner Mary Whitehouse calls for Chuck Berry's single 'My Ding a Ling' to be banned.

Mary Whitehouse

11th *Apollo 17* becomes the last of the *Apollo*s to land on the Moon.

15th **Bertolucci**'s *Last Tango in Paris*, starring Marlon Brando and Maria Schneider, is released in Paris.

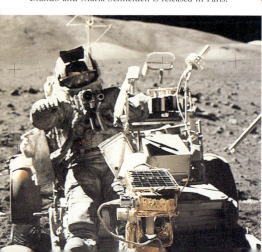

Apollo 17's Lunar Roving Vehicle

22nd Manchester United appoint former Scotland boss Tommy Docherty as their new manager.

23rd Andrei Tupolev, the great Russian aviation pioneer, dies, aged 84.

Marlon Brando in *Last Tango in Paris*

25th The third major earthquake this century destroys the Nicaraguan capital of Managua, killing up to 10,000.

29th 16 survivors of an aircraft that crashed in the Andes on 16 October have revealed the terrible secret of their survival. Faced with certain death from starvation when food ran out after just a few days, they ate the bodies of the dead.

Survivors of the Andes plane crash

Andrew Lloyd Webber and Tim Rice's stage musical, *Jesus Christ Superstar*, premieres in 1972.

1973

January 1973

5th Werner Herzog's South American epic *Aguirre Wrath Of The Gods* opens in Paris.

9th Former Velvet Underground singer Lou Reed marries Betty, a cocktail waitress, in New York.

11th The first Open University degrees are awarded to 867 students. More than half of the graduates – all of whom have earned exemptions from some parts of their syllabuses – are connected with teaching, though they also include a City bank clerk and a naval officer.

22nd Former US President Lyndon Johnson dies.

23rd President Nixon declares a cease-fire after the warring sides in the Vietnam crisis finally agree a truce. As a result, all US troops and personnel must leave Vietnam within 60 days, and political prisoners be freed.

 26th US actor Edward G. Robinson, star of films including *Key Largo* and *The Sea Wolf*, dies.

Signing the Peace Declaration to end the Vietnam War

30th Pan Am and TWA have scrapped their plans to buy 13 Concords, a major blow to the aircraft's future.

February 1973

1st The London Stock Exchange allows female traders on to the floor for the first time in history.

11th At Avoriaz's International Festival of Horror and Fantasy Films, Stephen Spielberg wins first prize – and professional recognition – for *Duel*.

14th David Bowie collapses from exhaustion at the end of a New York show.

14th British heavyweight boxer Joe Bugner is beaten by Muhammad Ali in Las Vegas.

22nd Israelis shoot down a Libyan airliner over Sinai, killing 74.

March 1973

Noel Coward, who died at his Jamaica home

26th British playwright and actor Sir Noel Coward dies. His works include the plays *Private Lives* and *Blithe Spirit* and the popular song 'Mad Dogs and Englishmen'. He also produced films based on his own scripts, such as *Brief Encounter*, and appeared in several others.

28th Marlon Brando rejects an Oscar in protest at Hollywood's treatment of American Indians.

31st In a grandstand finish, Red Rum pips Crisp to the post to win the Grand National in record time.

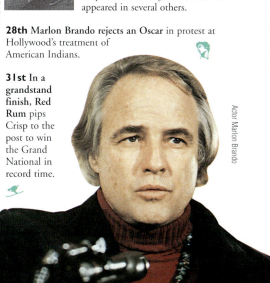

Actor Marlon Brando

April 1973

1st VAT replaces purchase tax to bring the UK in line with other Common Market countries.

8th Pablo Picasso dies, aged 91. The most prolific and influential artist of the twentieth century, Picasso embraced a number of artistic movements including Cubism and Surrealism. At the time of his death from a heart attack he was still working.

World-famous artist, Pablo Picasso

The new kings of rock, Queen

9th EMI launch their latest band, Queen, with a gig at London's Marquee Club.

May 1973

1st One-day strike by 1.6 million British union members in protest at the Tory pay freeze.

5th Second-Division Sunderland beat hot favourites Leeds 1–0 in the FA Cup final.

The award-winning journalists watch Nixon's speech

7th American journalists Bob Woodward and Carl Bernstein win the Pullitzer Prize for their Watergate investigation.

24th Two UK government ministers resign after admitting associating with prostitutes. The Prime Minister said there had been no security breaches or blackmail attempts and that the Lord Privy Seal Earl Jellicoe and defence under-secretary Lord Lambton were under secret-service surveillance.

Lord Lambton's television interview with Robin Day

June 1973

4th The Soviet Tupolev T144, an almost exact copy of Concord (nicknamed 'Concordski'), crashes at the Paris air show. All nine crew members die, nine spectators are killed and 28 are injured by falling debris. It is being treated as a case of pilot error.

5th David Bowie's *Aladdin Sane* tops the UK charts. The album features songs written during Bowie's first US tour.

7th A month after *Skylab* was launched, astronauts have fixed its broken solar panels making the vessel fully operational again.

16th The world premiere of Benjamin Britten's *Death In Venice* is staged at Snape Maltings, Suffolk.

Sweden's Bjorn Borg at Wimbledon

22nd The Wimbledon Tennis Championship is disrupted as players strike in support of a suspended Yugoslavian colleague.

22nd British architect John Poulson is questioned by police over allegations of building-contract corruption in the North of England.

25th President Nixon is accused of a leading role in concealing White House involvement in the Watergate burglary.

July 1973

Gary Glitter hits number 1 with 'I'm the leader of the gang'.

2nd US actress and former pin-up girl Betty Grable dies.

7th British racing driver **Roger Wilkinson dies** at the Dutch Grand Prix.

Idi Amin

9th Amin expels 112 members of the US **Peace Corps** following their two-day detention in Uganda.

13th In London, **David Bedford** knocks eight seconds off Lasse Virne's 10,000-metre world record.

Betty Grable in one of her most famous poses

19th **Kung fu film star Bruce Lee**, best known for *Enter the Dragon*, dies.

21st **France has joined the 'H-bomb club'** by setting off its own device in the South Pacific. Tiny Muraroa atoll was rocked by an explosion thought to be in the one-megaton range. There are now five nations with H-bombs.

Bruce Lee

30th **An 11-year legal battle** results in £20 million in compensation for the UK Thalidomide victims.

The skateboarding boom has arrived.

The BBC begins broadcasting *Last of the Summer Wine*.

August 1973

18th **West End stores Harrods and Libertys** are firebombed in attacks blamed on the IRA.

25th **The medical CAT scanner** is invented by English physicist Godfrey Hounsfield. The scanner enables doctors to look at a cross-section of the body's internal structure.

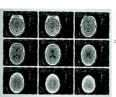

Brain scans

28th 180 soccer hooligans are arrested on the first day of the new football season.

31st **David Niven's highly entertaining autobiography**, *The Moon's A Balloon*, is the month's top-selling paperback. The quintessentially English actor is best known for his gentlemanly roles in films such as *A Matter of Life and Death*.

September 1973

Literary deaths: J. R. R. Tolkein, author of *Lord of the Rings*, dies aged 81 (3rd); the English poet W. H. Auden dies aged 66 (28th).

1st A new record for a deep-sea rescue has been set in the Atlantic. The tiny *Pisces 3* submarine spent 76 hours at a depth of 280 m (1,706 ft) before being brought to the surface. The rescue was carried out entirely by remote-control robots.

11th President Allende, the elected Marxist leader of Chile, is killed in a violent military coup.

Conrad Jnr. taking a bath on board *Skylab*

19th Former Byrds star Gram Parsons dies from a multiple drug overdose.

24th The second *Skylab* **crew return** safely to Earth after 59 days in space.

American pop group The Byrds

October 1973

6th **Egypt and Syria attack Israel** in what becomes known as the Yom Kippur War.

8th **UK Prime Minister Ted Heath** imposes a seven-per-cent ceiling on pay rises.

8th **London's first official commercial radio station** opens. The London Broadcasting Company, or LBC, have broken the BBC's 50-year monopoly and will broadcast 24-hour news and current affairs.

9th **Capital Radio**, London's second commercial station commences broadcasting.

Capital Radio DJs in the studio

PM Edward Heath singing the National Anthem

Elvis and Priscilla Presley in happier times

9th **Elvis and Priscilla Presley divorce.** They leave court with arms linked, kiss and go their separate ways.

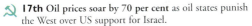

17th **Oil prices soar by 70 per cent** as oil states punish the West over US support for Israel.

22nd **Cellist Pablo Casals dies aged 96.** Born in Catalonia, Casals was a dedicated supporter of the Republicans during the Spanish Civil War. After they were defeated by General Franco, Casals refused to return to his homeland.

WILLS'S CIGARETTES

PABLO CASALS

28th **The Yom Kippur War** ends as a UN cease-fire comes into full effect. Israel fought back strongly, defeating Egypt and breaking the Syrian defences.

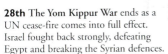

Jorn Utzon's spectacular Sydney Harbour Opera House is completed.

November 1973

1st The final issue of Richard Neville's satirical magazine *Oz* is published in the UK.

14th **Princess Anne marries Captain Mark Phillips** in a full military ceremony at Westminster Abbey.

16th *Skylab* is now producing some very interesting results from its space-based experiments, not least the effects of prolonged weightlessness on crew members. These do not appear to be as severe as first expected. The third crew has docked with the station, along with supplies for an extended mission.

Skylab Crew: Gerald Carr, Edward Gibson and William Pogue

December 1973

Film premieres; *Papillon*, starring Dustin Hoffman and Steve McQueen (17th); *The Exorcist* (26th).

14th John Paul Getty III, teenage grandson of the oil tycoon, is freed after being held by Italian kidnappers for six months. After posting his right ear to his family, the kidnappers demanded a ransom of $750,000.

20th Bobby Darin, who sang on hits like 'Mack The Knife', dies on the operating table.

31st David Bowie receives an award for having five different albums in the charts at the same time, for 19 weeks running.

John Paul Getty III

1974

January 1974

People in the UK start working a three-day week, as a result of industrial disputes.

2nd Encouraged by the Conservative Government, 18 of the UK's national museums and art galleries introduce entrance charges.

11th The world's first sextuplets to have all survived have been born in South Africa: three girls and three boys.

Brentfields oil rig, North Sea

12th Steve Miller's 'The Joker' tops the US charts.

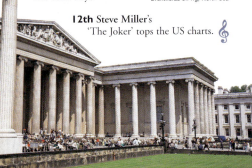

Summertime queues outside London's British Museum

25th A new approach to heart transplants occurred today when a man was fitted with a second heart to help out his own. The operation took place in South Africa and was performed by the world-renowned surgeon Dr Christiaan Barnard.

25th BP have announced another major oil find in the North Sea.

28th Muhammad Ali beats Smokin' Joe Frazier on points at Madison Square Garden.

Muhammad Ali knocked down by Joe Frazier

31st US film producer Samuel Goldwyn dies. As founder of the Metro Goldwyn Mayer Company he was among the greatest of the Hollywood moguls.

February 1974

5th Patty Hearst, 19-year-old daughter of millionaire publisher William Randolph Hearst, has been snatched from her San Francisco home and held hostage by abductors calling themselves the Symbionese Liberation Army. Brainwashing is feared after Patty is later heard on the ransom tape calling herself a 'prisoner of war'.

14th Russian authorities react to the publication of Solzhenitsyn's *The Gulag Archipelago*, by exiling him.

Solzhenitsyn (centre), the cause of much debate

24th A painting by the Dutch master Vermeer, valued at £1 million, is stolen from Kenwood House in London.

March 1974

6th **Third time unlucky** for PM Harold Wilson after Labour win power but not overall control.

20th **Princess Anne is shot at** but unhurt in a kidnap attempt. A gunman fired six shots at her car, with one bullet reportedly passing between her and husband Captain Mark Phillips. The gunman was arrested but only after seriously wounding four people, including the princess's bodyguard and chauffeur.

Harold Wilson: disapointed again

20th **Exhibitions by Minimalists** Yves Klein and Piero Manzoni open at the Tate Gallery in London.

29th **The US space probe** *Mariner 9* has taken the first close-up pictures of Mercury.

Princess Anne's bodyguard, James Beaton (centre)

Irish women flout the law by buying contraceptives

April 1974

1st A free family **planning service** is introduced as part of the UK's restructured National Health Service. In Eire, contraception remains illegal.

1st England and Wales undergo a reshuffle as change in local government leads to a redefining of county boundaries.

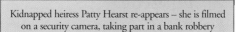

Kidnapped heiress Patty Hearst re-appears – she is filmed on a security camera, taking part in a bank robbery

3rd US President Nixon is billed for over $400,000 of unpaid income tax.

President Richard M. Nixon

5th The Mexican yacht *Sayula II* wins the Whitbread Round-the-World race.

13th End of a two-day strike in Japan. Over 6 million workers downed tools during the action.

17th The 1,000th victim of the Northern Ireland Troubles of the last five years dies.

23rd A coup takes place in Portugal, with the aim of replacing dictatorship with democracy.

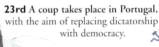

27th Denis Law scores for Manchester City, condemning his former club, Manchester United, to the Second Division for the first time ever.

Footballer Dennis Law

May 1974

There are reports that India has conducted its first atomic-bomb tests.

Abba are at number 1 with 'Waterloo', the song that won last month's Eurovision song contest.

1st It was officially announced **today** that Sir Alf Ramsey has been sacked as England manager. Time had been running out for Ramsey ever since the England team failed to qualify for the 1974 World Cup finals by losing to Poland in October 1973.

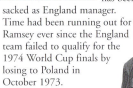

Swedish pop group Abba

11th The death toll in **China** is expected to exceed 20,000 after an earthquake rips through Sichuan and Yunnan.

20th The 500th episode of the UK TV series *Z Cars* is screened.

24th Francis Ford Coppola's film *The Conversation* wins the Grand Prix at the Cannes Film Festival.

25th US jazz musician **Duke Ellington**, who worked extensively with Ella Fitzgerald, dies.

Cartoon of Duke Ellington

26th Mass hysteria grips the audience at a David Cassidy concert: 1,000 fans need medical attention.

David Cassidy before the release of 'Tomorrow'

The latest *Encyclopaedia Britannica* goes on sale – it's the fifteenth edition.

June 1974

5th Singer Sly Stone marries Kathy Silva on stage at New York's Madison Square Garden.

10th A huge explosion at a chemical plant near Flixborough, Humberside kills 28 and injures many more. Scores of houses were destroyed by the explosion and there are fears the surrounding countryside may never recover.

22nd In the first Test in Cape Town the British Lions defeat South Africa 12–3.

30th Soviet ballet dancer Mikhail Baryshnikov has defected while touring in Toronto.

Remains of vehicles and fires at Flixborough

July 1974

Juan Perón

1st Argentine President Perón dies. His wife Isabel becomes the first woman president of a Latin American country.

7th West Germany beat Holland to win the World Cup.

21st The police introduce a national computer database. The Police National Computer, or PNC, will hold all details of criminal records, owners of cars and much more. The police have welcomed the new system despite accusations of 'Big Brother' tactics by civil-liberties groups.

The face of police computing in the 1990s

27th Blues star Lightnin' Slim dies of stomach cancer.

 29th Cass Elliott of the Mamas and the Papas dies aged 33.

August 1974

9th **President Nixon ducks impeachment** over the Watergate scandal by resigning. Gerald Ford, the Vice-President, automatically becomes the new President.

Panavia Tornado prototype 08

14th **The first flight** of the prototype of Tornado, the RAF's new multi-purpose strike aircraft.

16th The Soviets launch *Soyuz 15* into orbit safely.

16th **The overnight collapse** of the Horizons and Clarksons holiday group leaves 40,000 British holidaymakers stranded abroad.

US President Richard Nixon

Land artist Christo gives an interview

Bill Shankly with his victorious Liverpool side

19th The Bulgarian artist Christo, whose previous works include wrapping a section of Australian coastline and stringing a 13,000-square metre curtain across a valley in Colorado, 'wraps' the Ocean Front and a wall, at Newport Rhode Island, in white polypropylene for 18 days.

24th Liverpool's Bill Shankly announces his retirement and the £200,000 signature of Arsenal's Ray Kennedy simultaneously.

29th Hippies and police clash during an eight-hour battle at an illegal pop festival in Windsor.

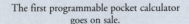

The first programmable pocket calculator goes on sale.

September 1974

Gillette launch a disposable safety razor that will eliminate the need to change blades.

4th British athletes Alan Pascoe, Steve Ovett and David Jenkins win gold medals at the European Championships.

12th Emperor Haile Selassie of Ethiopia is deposed in a coup after a reign of almost 60 years.

14th William Walton's seven-and-a-half-minute motet for unaccompanied mixed voices, *Cantico del Sole*, receives its British premiere at the BBC studios in Manchester.

Richard Nixon with his family

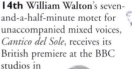

Sir William Walton on his 70th birthday

16th Shamed Nixon is granted a pardon by his successor despite suspicions of criminal activity over Watergate.

17th British nurses receive a pay increase of up to 58 per cent in the latest hefty wage hike since Labour won the election. In March, the miners ended their four-week strike after winning a 35 per cent rise. ☭

23rd Ceefax, the TV-based text-information service, transmits on BBC television for the first time. ☢

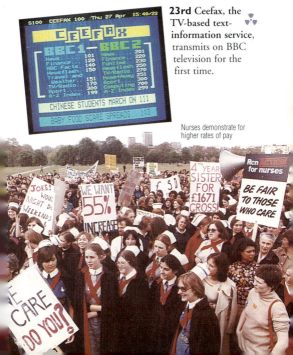

Nurses demonstrate for higher rates of pay

October 1974

1st The UK's first McDonald's hamburger restaurant opens in South London.

1st At Wembley, **John Conteh** defeats Jorge Ahumada to take the world light-heavyweight title.

11th The second general election in the UK this year secures a three-seat majority for Labour.

Argentina's Jorge Ahumada, waiting to fight John Conteh

15th Inmates riot at **Northern Ireland**'s notorious Maze Prison.

Rt. Hon. Harold Wilson, MP

25th English folk singer Nick Drake dies after an overdose of antidepressants. Drake was born in 1948 and began recording at the age of 19. His work includes *Five Leaves Left*, *Bryter Layter* and *Pink Moon*. The coroner later confirmed his death as suicide.

30th In Kinshasa, Zaire, Muhammad Ali defeats the 3–1 favourite George Foreman, becoming only the second man to regain the world heavyweight title. Forsaking his famous 'shuffle' Ali soaked up the best of Foreman's blows before knocking out the defending champion in the final round.

George Foreman knocked out in the final round

Lord Lucan, who has mysteriously disappeared

November 1974

12th Police launch a hunt for the missing seventh Earl of Lucan. Known as 'Lucky' to friends, he is the chief suspect after nanny Sandra Rivett is found battered to death at the Lucan family's Belgravia home. She was found by Lady Lucan who had also been attacked.

21st Peter Shilton becomes the world's most expensive goalkeeper, worth £340,000.

21st Two busy Birmingham pubs are bombed by IRA terrorists in the worst mainland atrocity to date. The simultaneous attacks killed 17 and injured 120.

26th Video-taped evidence has been used in a court of law for the first time.

December 1974

3rd The Glyndebourne production of Stravinsky's *The Rake's Progress*, with sets by David Hockney, opens.

10th In Stockholm, **Alexander Solzhenitsyn** finally accepts the Nobel Prize for Literature – which he was awarded in 1970. The author, who was forcibly exiled from the USSR to West Germany earlier in 1974, thanked the Swedish Assembly for honouring his empty chair during his absence.

Russian author
Alexander Solzhenitsyn

21st Glam-rock band Mud hit number 1 with 'Lonely This Christmas'.

24th British MP **John Stonehouse** materialises in Australia under a false passport. He vanished from a Miami beach a few weeks ago.

John Stonehouse

1975

January 1975

Bob Dylan releases *Blood on the Tracks*, his first album back on CBS. After a mixed start to the decade, it is Dylan's most consistent album since the mid-Sixties, containing classic tracks like 'Tangled Up In Blue'.

The Altair, the world's first home computer, goes on sale at $650.

2nd The world's second-largest oil company, Burmah Oil, collapses.

2nd Silent film star Charlie Chaplin is knighted in the New Year Honours.

The newly knighted Sir Charles Chaplin

Cambodian children pack into a makeshift trailer

4th Phnom Penh, Cambodia's capital, comes under heavy attack from Khmer Rouge guerrillas, led by Pol Pot. The US embassy plans to start an evacuation of American personnel.

9th In Melbourne, the Australian cricket team, inspired by bowlers Lillee and Thomson, regains the Ashes.

16th Angola gains independence after 400 years of Portuguese rule.

US and USSR spacecraft dock together in space for the first time.

February 1975

1st The first edition of a new computer language, known as BASIC, goes on sale. It is designed for ease of use rather than power and should bring computer programing within the reach of ordinary people.

5th The UK Government gives the go-ahead for two new nuclear power stations. Sizewell B is the only one to be built.

Margaret Thatcher

11th Margaret Thatcher beats an all-male opposition to become the first female leader of a British political party. She heads the Conservative Party.

Eamon de Valera

11th Hal Ashby's raunchy comedy, *Shampoo*, starring Warren Beatty and Julie Christie, opens in New York.

14th P. G. Wodehouse, creator of the comic aristocrat Bertie Wooster, dies aged 94.

Scene from the comedy, *Shampoo*

19th A boat powered entirely by solar energy is unveiled.

An early picture of P. G. Wodehouse and friends

Irish politician Eamon de Valera, who took part in the 1916 Easter Rising, dies in August of this year.

March 1975

The Bay City Rollers' 'Bye Bye Baby' knocks Telly Savalas's 'If' from the top of the UK charts.

 Professor Erno Rubik begins work on his puzzle cube – but does not patent the idea!

1st Mike Oldfield wins the Grammy for Best Instrumental Composition for *Tubular Bells*.

Mike Oldfield

7th **Lesley Whittle**, the kidnapped Shropshire heiress, is found strangled in a 60-foot drain shaft near a country park in Staffordshire, 52 days after being snatched from her home. The abductor, known only as the Black Panther, demanded a £50,000 ransom but didn't collect the money.

Professor Rubik puzzles over his cube

April 1975

3rd 23-year-old **Russian**, Anatoly Karpov, is the world's youngest chess champion – his opponent, Bobby Fisher, failed to meet the deadline for entry to the match.

5th Chiang Kai Shek, President of Nationalist China, dies.

Anatoly Karpov, the new chess champion

11th Legendary **dancer** and member of the Folies Bérgères, Josephine Baker, dies in Paris aged 68.

30th North **Vietnam captures Saigon**, the capital of South Vietnam, after nearly 20 years of fighting. Saigon will now be known as Ho Chi Minh City.

May 1975

 After a three-month siege at Phnom Penh, the communist Khmer Rouge are now in charge in Cambodia. Up to three million people are believed to have died so far.

Tammy Wynette's 'Stand By Your Man' tops the UK charts.

The Birmingham Six

2nd The six accused IRA Birmingham pub bombers are found guilty and jailed for 10 to 15 years.

5th The next generation of UK trains enters service between Paddington and Weston-super-Mare, a distance of 220 km (137 miles). The train can reach a speed of over 190 km/h (120 mph) over certain sections of track.

Technology keeps producing ever faster trains

14th Frank Sinatra wins substantial damages from the BBC. The case came about after allegations were made that Sinatra had links with the Mafia.

16th Climber Junko Tabai of Japan becomes the first woman to reach the top of Mount Everest.

22nd Barbara Hepworth, one of the UK's leading sculptors, dies in a studio fire, aged 72.

30th Gregg Allman and Cher get married – nine days later she files for divorce.

Sculptress Dame
Barbara Hepworth

June 1975

The Ramones and Talking Heads co-headline the Summer Rock Festival at New York club CBGBs.

5th **The Suez Canal** reopens after eight years.

6th **A British referendum** reveals 67.2 per cent are in favour of staying in the EEC.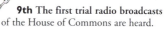

9th **The first trial radio broadcasts** of the House of Commons are heard.

12th **The Indian Prime Minister**, Indira Gandhi, is convicted of electoral fraud and her election to India's equivalent of the House of Commons, Lok Sabha, is annulled. Mrs Gandhi, who plans to appeal, was said to have had help in her election efforts from government officials.

Politician and former Prime Minister, Indira Gandhi

18th The first operational deliveries of North Sea oil take place.

21st At Lord's, the West Indies beat Australia to win the first cricket World Cup.

29th American folk singer Tim Buckley dies of a heroin overdose. He was considering playing Woody Guthrie on film around the time of his death.

July 1975

5th Arthur Ashe is Wimbledon's first black Men's Singles winner. He beat Jimmy Connors 6–1, 6–1, 5–7, 6–4.

11th 6,000 life-size terracotta statues are discovered by Chinese archaeologists. Found near the ancient city of Xi'an, it is thought they were made to guard the tomb of the Emperor Qin Shihuagdi who died in 206 BC.

The terracotta warriors

13th At Carnoustie, the 25-year-old American Tom Watson wins the British Open Golf Championship.

15th Stable lads return to work from an 11-week strike – their weekly wage is increased to £37.

August 1975

10cc's 'I'm Not in Love' rides high in the UK charts.

Vivienne Westwood and Malcolm McLaren

Malcolm McLaren and self-taught designer Vivienne Westwood are charged with a breach of public decency. The police raided their King's Road shop, Sex, and found T-shirts featuring pantless cowboys with their penises almost touching.

5th Dutch Elm disease has now struck down over three million trees in the UK.

12th In Gothenburg, Sweden, John Walker sets a new world record for running the mile: 3 mins, 49.4 seconds.

New Zealander, John Walker

September 1975

 Blue-collar American rocker Bruce Springsteen releases _Born to Run_.

9th Czech tennis star Martina Navratilova defects to the West.

11th An end of an era in UK car production as the last Wolseley is built.

Martina Navratilova

Wolseley saloon car on display in Paris

The last prisoners interned without trial, in August 1971, in Northern Ireland are released.

16th Christians and Muslims **clash** in bloody street battles as civil war decimates the Lebanese capital, Beirut.

22nd A female assassin attempts **to kill US President** Gerald Ford – it is Ford's second brush with death this month. Both would-be assassins have been female: the first was Lynette Fromme and the second, Sara Moore.

24th Dougal Haston and Doug Scott become the first to conquer Everest by the southwest face route.

30th In a gruelling **contest** Muhammed Ali beats Joe Frazier, to retain his world heavyweight title.

Fires and chaos on the streets of Beirut

Heavyweight boxer, Joe Frazier

October 1975

3rd In London's 'Spaghetti House Siege', seven Italian restaurant workers are freed unharmed after being held hostage in the basement. Their ordeal began on 28 September, when an armed robbery went wrong. Police refused to give in to the captors' demands.

Knightsbridge's Spaghetti House

5th **Austrian motor ace Niki Lauda**, driving for Ferrari, takes the Formula One World Championship.

9th **A bomb blast kills one person** and injures 20 outside Piccadilly's Green Park tube station.

 9th **Andrei Sakharov** is awarded the Nobel Peace Prize.

Princess Grace awarding the prizes at the Monaco Grand Prix

November 1975

3rd The first North Sea oil pipeline opens near Scotland, it it is over 376 km (235 miles) long.

10th Angola gains independence from Portugal; this is followed by fierce civil war, with 40,000 reported dead.

22nd King Juan Carlos reclaims the Spanish throne following the death of General Franco on 20 November.

King Juan Carlos and Queen Sophia of Spain

29th Twice Formula One World Champion Graham Hill, and five other members of his Grand Prix team, die when the plane that Hill was piloting, crashes in fog near Elstree Airport.

Formula One driver, Graham Hill

December 1975

1st Rock group **Queen** bring opera to the charts when 'Bohemian Rhapsody' reaches UK number 1.

7th Indonesian troops invade East Timor, newly independent from Portugal.

13th Malcolm Fraser leads the Liberal Party to election victory in Australia.

Freddie Mercury, lead singer of Queen

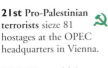

21st Pro-Palestinian terrorists sieze 81 hostages at the OPEC headquarters in Vienna.

26th 'Concordski' enters commercial service in the USSR.

Malcolm Fraser

1976

January 1976

2nd Winds of up to 168 km/h (105 mph) sweep the UK killing 22 people.

7th SAS troops are sent into the heart of sectarian violence boosting forces to 15,200 in Northern Ireland.

8th Chou En Lai dies – he was Premier of China since 1949.

10th Legendary Memphis bluesman Howlin' Wolf dies. He wrote 'Smokestack Lightnin' and 'Spoonful'.

12th The UK's wealthiest author, Dame Agatha Christie, dies aged 85. Famous for her 'whodunnits' and as the creator of the Belgian detective, Hercule Poirot, she wrote 85 books and 17 plays, including *The Mousetrap*, in a career that spanned half a century.

Dame Agatha Christie

15th **In Switzerland** British skater John Curry wins the men's European Figure Skating championship.

21st **Both the UK and French Concords** take off simultaneously on their first commercial flights.

22nd A mechanical 'bionic' arm has been fitted to Dr Gerald Shannon, a professor of engineering and a car crash victim in Queensland, Australia.

February 1976

2nd The Queen opens Birmingham's new National Exhibition Centre, built at a cost of £45 million.

24th A Navy gunboat heads into choppy waters as the fishing dispute between the UK and Iceland worsens. It is the third sent into the dispute so far.

'Cod War' gunboat surveyed by the Navy

18th Controversy surrounds the installation of the Tate Gallery's latest exhibit. *Equivalent VIII* is a work by Carl Andre made from 120 firebricks, laid out in two layers, in a rectangular shape. But, ask both critics and the public, is it art?

24th The artist L. S. Lowry, famous for his 'naive' industrial landscapes, dies aged 88.

London's Tate Gallery

March 1976

The world's first major home-computer convention has taken place in Alberquerqe, US. Arranged for users of the Altair home computer to swap ideas and programs, the convention was deemed a great success by its organisers, who hope to make it an annual event. In the same month Apple releases its first computer.

An early Apple computer

1st Bob Dylan's *Desire* tops the charts in the US.

16th Harold Wilson shocks the UK by resigning as Prime Minister; James Callaghan takes over.

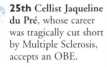 **25th** Cellist Jaqueline du Pré, whose career was tragically cut short by Multiple Sclerosis, accepts an OBE.

April 1976

Howard Hughes surrounded by the press

5th Reclusive US **billionaire**, film producer and industrialist Howard Hughes dies. Hughes also designed aircraft and broke several air-speed records. He spent the last 21 years of his life out of the public view.

25th British director Sir Carol Reed, whose films include *The Third Man*, dies aged 69.

26th British comedy actor Sid James collapses on stage and dies. Named *TV Times*' Funniest Man On Television in 1974, South African-born James starred in 19 *Carry On* films and appeared on television.

28th Mervyn Davies collapses during a Rugby Union Welsh Cup semi-final. He recovers in hospital.

Sir Carol Reed

May 1976

4th Liverpool win the Football League Championship for the record ninth time.

10th Liberal leader Jeremy Thorpe stands down after a male model claims they had a homosexual affair. The former party leader claims he has been forced out by a bigoted media witch hunt. He also denies the affair with Norman Scott. On 7 July, David Steel becomes leader.

27th The House of Commons is suspended in uproar when Michael Heseltine whirls the Mace around his head. It is caused by the Government's win – by one vote – on a crucial shipbuilding nationalisation bill.

MP Jeremy Thorpe

June 1976

 A study on endangered species published in the US concludes that, unless immediate measures are taken to protect the environment, over 4,000 species of animals will become extinct within the next 30 years!

Abba's 'Fernando' single and *Greatest Hits* album top the charts.

The Dorchester Hotel, Park Lane

18th **Three days of riots** in Soweto and other South African townships leave over 100 dead.

21st **Luxury London hotel**, the Dorchester, is sold for £9 million to two Arab buyers.

28th **The Seychelles** are granted independence, after 162 years of British rule.

July 1976

4th The US celebrates 200 years of independence.

10th A firing squad executes one American and three British mercenaries in war-torn Angola.

24th At the Olympics in Montreal, Canada, Britain's David Wilkie wins the 200 m breast stroke title and gives the UK its first swimming gold medal since 1908. Other British gold medallists include the three-man Modern Pentathlon team led by Adrian Parker.

29th Southend Pier suffers severe fire damage. There is a chance the pier, the world's longest, will have to be demolished.

Southend Pier before the fire

August 1976

Master of the suspense film, Fritz Lang

2nd German film director Fritz Lang, whose greatest achievement was the 1926 film *Metropolis*, dies.

6th Runaway Labour MP John Stonehouse is jailed for seven years for forgery and theft.

8th The Protestant and Catholic Woman's Peace Movement is launched in Northern Ireland and some 20,000 attend a rally in Belfast. The movement is a response to the increasing death toll. Three of the most recent victims were children.

11th British Leyland, the UK's main car and lorry manufacturer, is nationalised.

John Stonehouse MP

13th In the fifth Test against England at the Oval, West Indies batsman Viv Richards hits a record score of 291.

19th In a letter to *The Times*, artist Tom Keating claims to have forged several paintings attributed to the Victorian painter, and acolyte of William Blake, Samuel Palmer. Keating was moved to write as a protest against the dealers who make a handsome profit from his forgeries.

Antigua-born cricketer, Viv Richards

24th In one of the hottest, driest summers the UK has ever seen, a Minister for Drought is appointed, Denis Howell. Three days later it starts raining!

Tom Keating's self-portrait

September 1976

3rd The second of the *Viking* space probes touched down on the surface of Mars today. *Viking II* will continue to survey the surface of the planet and analyse samples for traces of life. Scientists are still hopeful of this despite the negative results from the first *Viking* mission in July.

9th The 800 million inhabitants of Communist China are in mourning after Chairman Mao Tse-tung (founder of the Chinese Communist Party and author of the *Little Red Book*) dies, aged 82. A fierce power struggle is already under way.

15th Nagisa Oshima's steamy film *Ai No Corrida* finally goes on censored release in Japan.

20th–21st A punk festival, arranged by Malcolm McLaren, is held at Oxford Street's 100 Club. Artists include the Clash and the Sex Pistols.

Punks in London's Trafalgar Square

October 1976

Commuters at London's Victoria Station

4th British rail **introduce** the HS125 train, the world's fastest diesel locomotive.

15th The Sex Pistols sign to EMI. A spokesman describes them as 'a group with a bit of guts for young people to identify with'.

23rd The 'Gang of Four', led by Chairman Mao's widow, are arrested for plotting to take over power in China.

Johnny Rotten of the Sex Pistols

Microsoft is founded by 19-year-old Bill Gates.

The Ecology Party is founded.

24th James Hunt wins the Formula One world title after Niki Lauda retires from the Japanese Grand Prix.

26th The UK's new £16-million National Theatre opens three years behind schedule. It was started in 1969 and is still not totally complete.

November 1976

2nd **Democrat Jimmy Carter** beats Republican rival Gerald Ford in the US presidential election.

6th **A Soviet defector** has revealed that a large nuclear accident occurred in the USSR in 1958.

16th **A record £8-million deposit-box robbery** at the Bank of America, Mayfair, lands eight in jail.

The Bank of England reviews its security policy after the Mayfair robbery

Jimmy Carter celebrates with Walter Mondale

Second Division Southhampton beat Manchester United 1–0 in the FA Cup Final.

Set and cast of *The Mousetrap*

17th London's St Martin's Theatre stages the 10,000th performance of Agatha Christie's *The Mousetrap*. The play, which revolves around a group of people, one of them a murderer, isolated in a snowbound house, was first performed in 1952, with Richard Attenborough in the leading role.

17th China has detonated another H-Bomb. Sources claim it is in the multi-megaton range.

26th Catholicism is no longer the official state religion of Italy.

27th The four-millionth Mini has been produced making it the biggest-selling UK-designed car by far.

A Mini test model

December 1976

 New York film premieres: *Bound For Glory* (5th), *King Kong* (18th) and *A Star is Born* (18th).

Model of King Kong at the World Trade Centre

3rd An attempt is made on reggae singer Bob Marley's life at his home in Kingston, Jamaica. Marley, who with his backing band The Wailers has brought reggae to the world, is shot, as are his wife and manager. None are killed but all are wounded; the attack happened during the country's general-election campaign.

3rd The Sex Pistols cause havoc on the set of the live UK TV programme *Today*.

4th In Switzerland, a proposal to shorten the official working week to 40 hours is rejected by the people.

The king of reggae, Bob Marley

BOB

5th After a long period of ill health, the composer Benjamin Britten dies peacefully in Aldeburgh, Suffolk.

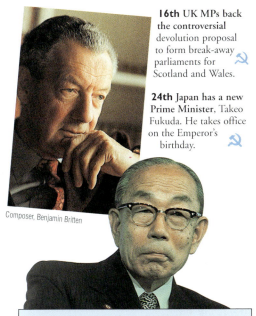

16th UK MPs back the controversial devolution proposal to form break-away parliaments for Scotland and Wales.

24th Japan has a new Prime Minister, Takeo Fukuda. He takes office on the Emperor's birthday.

Composer, Benjamin Britten

The last episode of *Dixon of Dock Green* is screened.

1977

January 1977

Bay City Rollermania reaches the US as their teenage American female fans greet them in tartan flares.

6th EMI sack the Sex Pistols because of their outrageous behaviour and the adverse publicity they have attracted.

9th 'Charter 77' is signed by 240 prominent Czechs calling for civil rights.

10th Inventor Clive Sinclair launches his new 5 cm (2 in) screen television. The sets will sell for £175.

10th It was claimed today that the Acropolis in Greece is being rapidly destroyed by pollution. The United Nations has launched an appeal to rescue the site, which

14th Former British PM, Anthony Eden, dies. ☭

17th Double murderer Gary Gilmore goes before a firing squad: the first US execution for 10 years.

22nd France win the Rugby Union **Grand Slam** without conceding a try or changing their side.

Murderer Gary Gilmore

23rd Brian De Palma's *Carrie*, starring Sissy Spacek, wins the Grand Prix at the Avoriaz Film Festival.

February 1977

Fleetwood Mac release their new album *Rumours*.

2nd The Pompidou Centre, jointly designed by Richard Rogers (UK) and Renzo Piano (Italy), opens in Paris to a mixed reception. Home of the city's contemporary art collection, the controversial building is in the heart of the eighteenth-century Marais quarter.

10th IRA terrorists are jailed for life for the six-day Balcombe Street siege in 1975.

17th The UK Government provides £6 million for research into solar power.

18th Archbishop of Uganda, Janani Luwum, is murdered at the instigation of Idi Amin, as the violence of Amin's rule increases.

Paris' controversial Pompidou Centre

March 1977

1st Leo Sayer tops the charts with 'When I Need You'.

Chart-topper Leo Sayer

17th Alan Ayckbourn's specially commissioned play, *Bedroom Farce*, opens at the new National Theatre.

17th Australia beat England by 45 runs in the centenary Test match in Melbourne.

27th Two jumbo jets – one Pan Am and one KLM owned – collide in fog on a Tenerife runway killing 574 in a fireball. Over 70 people survived the horrific accident and were hurried to nearby hospitals, mostly for burns treatment.

April 1977

2nd Tommy Stack rides Red **Rum** to a record hat-trick of Grand National wins.

15th Fugitive train robber Ronnie Biggs is a party guest on board a Royal Navy ship in Brazil. UK media outrage ensues.

19th After a hard-fought trial, the US Supreme Court decides that the spanking of school children should be allowed to continue.

Ronnie Biggs in Brazil

22nd The first fibre-optic telephone cables have gone into service in California, US. The 8.8 km (5½ mile) cable runs between Long Beach and Artemesia and has already handled 24 calls simultaneously, a significant improvement over conventional cables. ☢

26th Polaroid demonstrates its new instant cine film; Polavision can be viewed just 90 seconds after shooting. ☢

Filming *Rocky*

28th *Rocky*, written by and starring Sylvester Stallone, wins two Oscars: for Best Film and Best Director.

Revolutionary cine cameras are launched

30th In the North Sea, an oil slick of some 1,600 square km (1000 square miles) is spreading from the *Bravo* oil rig, eight days after it exploded.

May 1977

The Sex Pistols sign their third record deal in six months with Virgin – they have been dropped by both EMI and A&M. Virgin agree to release their new single 'God Save The Queen'.

10th US actress Joan Crawford dies. In what was really two Hollywood careers, Crawford moved from roles casting her as a working-class girl bettering herself, to darker parts in films like *Mildred Pierce* and *Whatever Happened to Baby Jane*.

13th The exiled Communist, Dolores Ibarruri, dubbed 'La Passionara' during the Spanish Civil War, comes home to Spain after 38 years.

13th Australian tycoon Kerry Packer has signed up over 30 top international cricketers to play in a series of matches in Australia.

15th Liverpool beat Borussia Moechengladbach 3–1 to take football's European Cup in Rome.

19th The Kenyan government bans 'big game' hunting.

29th Nigel Short, aged 11, becomes the youngest player to qualify for a national chess championship.

Media giant Kerry Packer

June 1977

Hewlett Packard have announced an electronic calculator small enough to be worn like a watch.

3rd **Roberto Rossellini**, Italian film director and former husband of Ingrid Bergman, dies.

4th **Jubilant Scottish football fans** dig up the pitch at Wembley after beating England 2-1.

4th **British artist Francis Bacon** turns down the award of the Companionship of Honour.

The late Roberto Rossellini

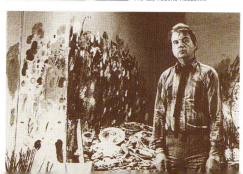

aArtist Francis Bacon in his

6th **The Queen** lights a bonfire in Windsor Great Park to begin a seven-day celebration of her 25 years on the throne. More than 100 other bonfires are lit across the UK ahead of tomorrow's thanksgiving service at St Paul's Cathedral.

11th 'God Save the Queen' by the Sex Pistols tops the UK charts despite an airplay ban.

15th **Democratic voting** takes place in Spain for the first time in 41 years.

16th **Werner von Braun**, creator of the modern space rocket, dies.

Werner von Braun

The Queen celebrates 25 years on the throne

July 1977

1st Virginia Wade wins the Women's Singles title at the 100th Wimbledon tennis tournament.

1st Industries in countries of the two separate European economic alliances, EEC and EFTA, are now free to trade with each other.

2nd Vladimir Nabokov, the Russian author of *Lolita, Pale Fire* and *Ada,* dies in the US aged 78.

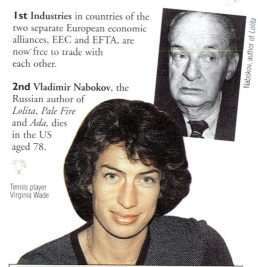

Nabokov, author of *Lolita*

Tennis player
Virginia Wade

Two homosexual men in New York are diagnosed with a rare cancer – they are later believed to have been the first-known victims of AIDS.

5th **Pakistani Prime Minister** Zulfikar Ali Bhutto is under arrest after being deposed by the man he made his army's Chief of Staff, Zia ul-Huq. The military take-over ends the general unrest that has gripped Pakistan over the last four months and has left hundreds dead.

New York City

13th **A power cut in New York** causes chaos. Shops and homes are raided by thieves as the city is plunged into blackness.

21st **Libya and Egypt** are at war over 'shared' territory. On the same day, Somalia invades Ethiopia.

22nd **The Chinese Communist Party** expels the infamous 'Gang of Four'.

The deposed Pakistani Prime Minister

August 1977

10th The Queen makes her first official visit to Northern Ireland for 11 years.

11th Geoff Boycott clocks up his 100th century in first-class cricket, against Australia at Headingly.

A triumphant Geoff Boycott

16th Elvis Presley, probably the most influential singer in popular music is found dead. Presley started out in the 1950s blending black and white styles – rhythm and blues and country and western – on classics like 'Heartbreak Hotel' and 'All Shook Up'. He appeared in a series of musical films and then relaunched himself as a lounge singer in the 1970s before drug addiction and overeating took their toll.

Voyager 2: destination Jupiter

17th The Soviet nuclear-powered ice-breaker *Arktika* becomes the first ship to reach the North Pole.

19th US comedian Groucho Marx dies.

20th The US *Voyager 2* space probe has been launched on its way towards Jupiter.

31st Rhodesia's majority white electorate sweep Ian Smith to victory with an 80 per cent vote.

Rhodesian premier
Ian Smith in LA

The sci-fi adventure film *Star Wars* is released.

September 1977

Steve Biko

12th **Civil-rights leader Steve Biko** is killed in police custody. The death, aged 30, of the leading light for South African blacks prompts a mass outpouring of grief among supporters, which peaks two weeks later, when a crowd of 15,000 mourners pack the streets for his funeral.

16th **Glam rock star Marc Bolan, of T. Rex fame, dies** in a car crash in South-West London. He was 29 years old. The driver, his girlfriend Gloria Jones, survives.

16th **Opera singer, Maria Callas**, dies of a heart attack at her home in Paris, aged 53.

19th **US film director Roman Polanski** is sentenced to three months in jail after having sex with a 13-year-old girl.

Glam rock star Marc Bolan

October 1977

4th Ballet star, **Rudolph Nureyev,** makes his debut as a film actor in Ken Russell's *Valentino*. The film is based on the life story of one of Hollywood's biggest stars of the Twenties, Rudolph Valentino. The tragic death of cinema's most idolised star, in 1926, caused several fans to attempt suicide.

8th London's **body count reaches 800** as striking undertakers call a halt to burials.

14th US entertainer Harry 'Bing' Crosby dies.

20th Two black **newspapers are banned** in South Africa as the authorities impose restrictions on press freedom.

The legendary 'Bing' Crosby

November 1977

15th **Princess Anne gives birth** to a 3.5 kg (7 lb 9 oz) son, Peter.

16th **Steven Spielberg's alien** abduction adventure *Close Encounters Of The Third Kind* opens in New York.

24th **Rhodesian premier Ian Smith** will give blacks a voice and end white rule. Smith has been undergoing negotiations with black leaders for several weeks now.

25th **Kerry Packer's 'Cricket Circus'** wins its High Court case against the established cricket authorities. The authorities had threatened to ban all players who had signed for Packer from playing Test cricket.

Kerry Packer

December 1977

3rd Desperate 'boat people' flee South Vietnam, and its new Communist rule, in their thousands.

12th The UK's fiercely conservative Jockey Club agrees to admit women as members.

15th A legend is born in New York with the release of *Saturday Night Fever*. The story focuses largely on the disco culture of America's youth. The main protagonist is played by rising acting and dancing star John Travolta.

Charlie Chaplin, star of the silver screen

25th Charlie Chaplin dies in Switzerland, aged 88.

Vietnamese evacuees dubbed 'boat people'

1978

January 1978

🎵 'Mull of Kintyre' by Wings tops the UK charts; the Bee Gees' *Saturday Night Fever* soundtrack tops the US charts.

1st Donald Woods, newspaper editor and champion of the late, black-consciousness leader, Steve Biko, escapes from house arrest in South Africa. After losing his police 'minders', Woods hitch-hikes north before finally swimming to freedom in Lesotho.

14th Johnny Rotten quits the Sex Pistols during an American tour.

15th In Pakistan, Geoff Boycott takes over from Mike Brearley as England's cricket captain.

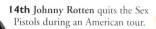

New England cricket captain, Geoff Boycott

12th Middlesbrough FC midfield player, Graham Souness, signs to Liverpool for the record fee of £352,000.

24th A Soviet satellite goes out of control and crash-lands in a remote part of Canada.

29th Sweden becomes the first country to legislate against CFC (chlorofluorocarbons) gases in aerosols. CFCs are known to cause damage to the ozone layer.

The Sex Pistols on stage

Trainers now account for 50 per cent of US shoe sales.

February 1978

13th ITN's first female newsreader, Anna Ford, starts work.

15th Leon Spinks becomes the first man to take the world heavyweight boxing title from Muhammed Ali.

24th Anthropologist Richard Leakey announces he has discovered evidence that man's ancient ancestors actually walked upright. A series of fossilised footprints have been uncovered in East Africa: they were made by two upright individuals walking across mud. The prints are thought to be around four million years old.

Anna Ford, first lady of ITN

March 1978

2nd Grave robbers steal the body of Charlie Chaplin – in May it is found buried 16 km (10 miles) away.

30th The Conservative Party employ Saatchi and Saatchi, the first advertising agency it has used since the 1950s. With a general election just around the corner, the Tories opt for US-style tactics and rather than rely on volunteers, they turn to the young, flashy Saatchi brothers instead.

4th The Welsh Rugby Union side take the Grand Slam in Cardiff, beating France 16–7.

24th The stricken oil tanker *Amoco Cadiz* has split into two, spilling 50,000 tons of oil into the English Channel.

April 1978

Radio broadcasts of the House of Commons are to become permanent.

3rd In **Hollywood,** Woody Allen's *Annie Hall* wins 4 Oscars: for Best Film, Best Director, Best Original Screenplay and Best Actress (Diane Keaton). The film features the director in the leading male role.

7th President Carter announces that production of the neutron bomb is to be postponed indefinitely.

President Jimmy Carter

Soap opera *Dallas* hits TV screens and *Superman* hits the big screen.

15th A hunt is launched for UK runaway Joyce McKinney, who abducted and sexually tormented a Mormon missionary. She kept him captive in her home.

22nd Brian Clough's Nottingham Forest win the First Division title in their first season after promotion.

24th ITV's *Upstairs Downstairs* is the first foreign TV programme to win the top US TV award, the Peabody.

25th Soviet leader Brezhnev follows Carter's lead and bans the neutron bomb.

27th A Soviet-backed coup seizes power in Afghanistan.

Joyce McKinney

The Cast of the award-winning *Upstairs Downstairs*

The first camera with automatic focus goes on sale.

May 1978

9th Italy's five-times **Prime Minister**, Aldo Moro's, rug-wrapped corpse is discovered in the back of a Renault in Rome. He had been shot. He was abducted by Red Brigade terrorists on 16 March.

Aldo Moro

10th **Princess Margaret** seeks a divorce from the Earl of Snowdon, two years after their separation.

13th Boney M are at number 1 with 'Rivers of Babylon'.

30th **The Ryder Cup**, traditionally a competition between golfers from the British Isles and the US, is opened to other European golfers.

30th **Liverpool FC win the European Cup** for the second year running, beating FC Bruges 1–0.

Princess Margaret's former husband, the Earl of Snowdon

June 1978

16th **The Taito Corporation** demonstrate a new kind of computer game in Tokyo – Space Invaders is born!

19th **All-rounder Ian Botham** takes eight wickets and scores a century against Pakistan at Lord's.

24th **A dozen British men**, women and children are massacred at an isolated mission as the Rhodesian bush war escalates.

24th **US astronomers** claim to have discovered the first Black Hole. These have been postulated for some time but without any hard evidence. The new find in the constellation Scorpio, has caused great excitement in the scientific community.

Botham: the toast of English cricket

July 1978

11th A gas explosion in the centre of a Spanish campsite kills 188 holidaymakers and leaves 200 more horrifically injured.

26th Louise Brown was born today weighing a healthy 2.6 kg (5 lbs 12 oz). She is the world's first test-tube baby, a technique developed for over a decade by Professor Patrick Steptoe and Dr Michael Edwards. Media interest is enormous and the rights to Louise's story have been sold for £300,000.

28th National Lampoon's anarchic, college-set film comedy, *Animal House*, starring John Belushi, opens in New York.

31st A solar-powered car has been demonstrated today near Rugby – it developed 0.2 horsepower!

John Belushi, star of *Animal House*

August 1978

August 11–17th The US gas balloon *Double Eagle* is the first to cross the Atlantic Ocean. The voyage took its three airmen six days to complete. The balloon took off from Maine and landed near Paris – in total it covered 5,120 km (3,200 miles).

22nd Jomo Kenyatta, who led Kenya to independence in 1963, dies.

25th Millions are expected at the first public exhibition of the Turin shroud for 45 years.

26th The newly elected Pope honours his two predecessors by taking the name Pope John Paul I.

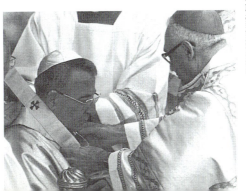

Under wraps: the Turin shroud revealed

September 1978

The *Grease* soundtrack tops the US LP charts. Originally an off-Broadway musical, the film version achieved world-wide success through songs such as the title track and 'You're the One That I Want'.

10th Sweden's Ronnie Petersen dies during the Italian Grand Prix after an accident involving James Hunt.

15th Muhammed Ali makes history when he wins the world heavyweight championship for the third time.

Disco culture is sweeping the western world.

18th Peace at last with the historic Israeli-Egyptian pact, the Camp David Agreement. Hopes for the future are high as Anwar Sadat, President of Egypt, and Israeli premier, Menachem Begin, are finally ready to put pen to paper on the peace agreement. US President Jimmy Carter fought tirelessly to keep the talks going.

20th A manhunt is launched after a 13-year-old newspaper boy, Carl Bridgewater, is found shot dead in a Staffordshire farmhouse.

29th BBC broadcaster Georgi Markov dies after being assassinated in a fatal stabbing – the weapon was a poisoned umbrella tip.

Georgi Markov

October 1978

12th **Ex-Sex Pistol Sid Vicious** is charged with the murder of his girlfriend Nancy Spungen.

16th **A Polish Cardinal**, Karol Wojtyla, is elected Pope after Pope John Paul I dies on his 33rd day in office. The first non-Italian Pope since 1542, he takes the title John Paul II.

18th **Anatoly Karpov** defeats Viktor Korchnoi in the World Chess Championship final in Baguio, Philippines.

17th **The Greenpeace vessel** *Rainbow Warrior* successfully prevents the annual grey-seal cull in Canada. The ship blocked access to other vessels and the crew stopped the hunters gaining access to the baby seals; the animals are killed for their fur.

November 1978

4th **Shoppers clear shops**' shelves of bread as the UK bakers' strike sparks a wave of panic buying.

18th 'Rat Trap' by Irish band Boomtown Rats (fronted by Bob Geldof) tops the charts.

29th **Investigators discover 913 bodies** littering the Guyanan jungle commune home of the People's Temple, a US religious cult led by the dictatorial fanatic Reverend Jim Jones.

Surviving members were found hiding, and claimed that Jones forced followers to swallow a cyanide-laced drink.

Queuing for bread as bakers strike

Microsoft's founder,
Bill Gates

December 1978

Microsoft sales top $1 million for the first time ever.

8th Golda Meir, former Prime Minister of Israel, dies.

10th Millions of men, women and children take to the streets in a non-violent demonstration as calls for the abdication of the Shah of Iran grow louder. Instead they want the return of Ayatollah Khomeini, exiled for 14 years.

10th Isaac Beshevis Singer wins the Nobel Prize for Literature.

A non-violent demonstration turns violent in Tehran

Former Liberal leader
Jeremy Thorpe, with his wife

13th Former Liberal leader Jeremy Thorpe faces trial over an alleged plot to murder male model Norman Scott.

15th Phillips launch the **Videodisc**: an LP-sized disc that can hold a whole film.

19th The FA bans former England manager Don Revie from all football management for 10 years: Revie had accepted an overseas job before resigning as manager of England.

30th It has been decided that Lee Harvey Oswald, John F. Kennedy's killer, did not act alone. The US House of Representatives now deems a second gunman was present.

Banned football boss Don Revie

Chairman Mao's *Little Red Book* is denounced by the Chinese media.

1979

January 1979

Atari launch their 800 series computer, capable of both games and semi-serious computing.

Miniature flat-screen TV is patented in Japan by Matsushita.

The Rubik's Cube goes on sale. Amazingly Erno Rubik has still not patented his idea.

Britain goes Rubik's Cube crazy

The Village People's Disco anthem 'YMCA' tops the charts.

The Shah of Iran is forced into exile by supporters of Ayatollah Khomeini.

23rd Space Invaders reaches the UK and visitors to amusement arcades go crazy.

30th White Rhodesians **approve** a new constitution that will lead to a black-dominated government.

31st Now is the winter of **Britain's discontent.** Unofficial strikes over the government's pay-restraint policy – which limits rises to five per cent – continue to freeze services with rubbish piles growing higher, hospitals turning away patients, bodies going unburied and hundreds of thousands of people laid off work.

Rubbish is piled high due to strikes

February 1979

Blondie, fronted by the charismatic Debbie Harry, are at number 1 with 'Heart of Glass'.

A fragment of a Soviet satellite crashlands on an Eastbourne golf course.

1st Ecstatic Iranians welcome back the Ayatollah Khomeini from exile, weeks after driving out the Shah.

The Ayatollah returns from exile

2nd Ex-Sex Pistol Sid Vicious dies from a heroin overdose. Vicious had just been released from prison before a trial for the murder of his former girlfriend Nancy Spungen. He had already attempted suicide following his arrest and the demise of the Pistols.

9th Trevor Francis becomes the UK's first £1-million football player; moving from Nottingham Forest to Birmingham City.

13th French-born US film director **Jean Renoir**, whose films included *La Grande Illusion*, dies.

Trevor Francis

Jean Renoir

13th IBM introduce the modem system, allowing computers to exchange data over telephone lines.

March 1979

Jupiter as seen by Voyager 1

Gloria Gaynor's 'I Will Survive' knocks Elvis Costello's 'Oliver's Army' from UK number 1.

7th *Voyager 1* has sent back amazing pictures of Jupiter. The colour photographs show the mysterious 'Red Spot' to be a whirling storm thousands of kilometres across. The photographs also clearly show several rings surrounding the planet similar to those around Saturn.

17th Wales win Rugby Union's Triple Crown for the third year running.

28th In London, Labour lose a vote of no confidence and a general election is called for 3 May.

29th Idi Amin is on the run. The Ugandan dictator's ruthless tyranny comes to an end as he flees from the capital Kampala to a northern hide-out with a few faithful troops. Amin launched his murderous regime by ousting President Obote eight years ago.

30th Known IRA target, Tory MP Airey Neave, is killed by a car bomb while leaving the House of Commons car park.

31st Pregnant women and children are evacuated after a leak at Three Mile Island nuclear power station, Pennsylvania.

Security is stepped up after the IRA bomb

Three Mile Island, Pennsylvania

April 1979

Pol Pot, executor of a murderous regime

2nd The horrific truth behind **Pol Pot's Khmer Rouge** begins to dawn after 2,000 weighted skeletons are found in a Cambodian lake, near Phnom Penh. Shallow forest graves piled with skulls and bones are also found. Many fear the grim discovery is merely the tip of the iceberg.

4th Mass murderer, the **Yorkshire Ripper**, takes the life of a non-prostitute as his grisly total reaches 11.

18th US actor Lee **Marvin** is told to pay $104,000 palimony to former lover Michelle Triola Marvin.

Lee Marvin

A jubilant Margaret Thatcher

May 1979

4th Margaret Thatcher, a 53-year-old grocer's daughter from Grantham, becomes the UK's first female Prime Minister. Thatcher promised a complete transformation of the British industrial and economic climate, including sweeping trade-union reform. The new Tory government has a majority of 43.

18th Karen Silkwood, a dead nuclear worker, has posthumously won $10.5 million in the US after being contaminated with radiation.

27th Queues for petrol mount up on garage forecourts as the political upheaval in Iran pushes fuel prices up elsewhere.

29th Methodist bishop Abel Muzorewa takes his oath as the first black Prime Minister of Zimbabwe.

June 1979

6th Chuck Berry is sentenced to five months in jail for tax evasion.

11th US cowboy actor John Wayne (born Marion Morrison) dies of cancer aged 72.

12th The *Gossamer Albatross*, an entirely man-powered aircraft, succeeds in crossing the English Channel.

Chuck Berry

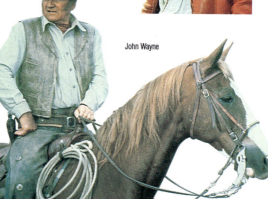

John Wayne

Carter and Brezhnev sign the SALT treaty

18th President Carter claims 'victory for peace' as he and Brezhnev sign the SALT arms limitations treaty.

23rd Inspired by Viv Richards, the West Indies win the Prudential World Cup at Lord's.

26th Muhammad Ali **announces his retirement** from boxing. It is the end of a controversial and sometimes glorious career during which Ali (aka Cassius Clay) converted to Islam, won the heavyweight title three times and was imprisoned for his refusal to go to the Vietnam War.

Boxing legend Muhammad Ali

UK television sees the adaptation of John Mortimer's *Rumpole of the Bailey* for the first time.

July 1979

Skylab has burnt up in the Earth's atmosphere, nearly seven years after its launch.

1st The Sony **Walkman**, a portable cassette player, goes on sale in Japan. It retails for $165 or Y33,000.

16th Iraq has a new president; his name is Saddam Hussein.

17th Nicaraguan dictator Anastasio **Somoza** seeks political asylum in the US, having been overthrown by the Marxist Sandanistas.

20th Despite an erratic performance, Spanish golfer Sevy Ballesteros wins the British Open. He is 22 years old. Ballasteros was playing against, among others, the current champion, Jack Nicklaus.

23rd The UK Cabinet approves cuts of £4,000 million (£1,000 million more than originally planned) in public spending, putting one civil service job in 10 in danger. Chancellor Sir Geoffrey Howe warns no cutbacks would spell economic and social disorder for Britain.

Saddam Hussein

The US Surgeon General publishes a major report confirming that smoking causes lung cancer.

August 1979

9th Brighton becomes the first British resort to open a special area for nude bathers near to the town centre. The decision marked a victory for local grandmother and nude-bathing fan Eileen Jakes who had long campaigned for a nudist area.

14th The Fastnet Race, traditionally the last competition of the Cowes Week yacht festival, is hit by disaster when hurricane-force winds wreck 25 of the 335 boats, killing 14 people, on the 100-mile course between Cornwall and the southern tip of Ireland.

Brighton, site of the UK's first naturist beach

Sebastian Coe

15th Sebastian Coe caps a glorious six weeks by setting a new 1,500 metres world record. He now holds three concurrent records: 800 metres, 1,500 metres and the mile.

15th The US Ambassador to the UN resigns over allegations of dealings with the PLO.

19th Two Soviet cosmonauts return to Earth after a record 175 days in space.

27th An IRA bomb rips through Lord Louis Mountbatten's boat, killing him and three others. War hero Mountbatten was also godfather to Prince Charles.

Lord Mountbatten's funeral

September 1979

Motorola release the 68,000 series microchip, which adds new power to Apple computers.

26th A fresh fight begins in Cambodia as the Red Cross and UNICEF lead the battle to save millions from death and starvation. A massive operation to fly in essential food and medical supplies gets clearance from the country's ruling party as well as the Khmer Rouge, which still controls some areas.

27th British actress and entertainer Dame Gracie Fields dies.

30th Pope John Paul II calls for peace as his first visit to Ireland unites all at an outdoor service.

October 1979

Quirky single 'Video Killed the Radio Star' is at number 1 for Buggles.

2nd Police step up the hunt for the Yorkshire Ripper with the launch of a £1 million publicity drive. The serial killer's reign of terror has seen the brutal killings of 12 women, most of whom were prostitutes. The police campaign includes the use of postmarks asking for public help – the first time this tactic has been used.

26th Park Chung Hee, the President of South Korea, is assassinated by his own Secret Service organisation.

30th Sir Barnes Wallis dies.

The late President of South Korea

November 1979

UK scientist Godfrey Hounsfield wins the Nobel Prize for inventing the medical CAT scanner.

4th Nearly 100 Americans are taken hostage after Iranian fanatics overpower guards at the US embassy in Tehran.

12th After a year of strikes prevented its publication, *The Times* newspaper reappears on the news-stands.

Noble prize-winner Godfrey Hounsfield

Demonstrators outside the besieged US embassy, Iran

Life of Brian banned in South Carolina

21st In a shock announcement in the House of Commons, it is revealed that Sir Anthony Blunt, the art adviser to the Queen, was the mysterious 'fourth man' in the infamous spy ring that also included Burgess, Philby and MacLean. Blunt is immediately stripped of his knighthood.

23rd After one screening, Monty Python's *The Life of Brian* is cancelled in Columbia, South Carolina – it is deemed blasphemous.

Sir Anthony Blunt, 'fourth man' in the spy ring

23rd A three-day siege at the Grand Mosque in Mecca ends when Saudi troops move in. The protesters were demonstrating against the Saudi Arabian political system.

30th 50,000 workers at British Steel are to lose their jobs as the recession worsens.

December 1979

Star Trek premiered in New York

New York film premieres: *Star Trek* (8th), *Kramer vs Kramer* (19th), *Being There* (20th) and *All That Jazz* (20th).

3rd On a tour of the US, British band The Who play Cincinatti, Ohio. Tragically, 11 people die and 28 are injured in the crush.

7th After Irish Prime Minister Jack Lynch's resignation on the 5th; Charles Haughey becomes the new Prime Minister.

The Who in the 1960s

12th **It has been decided** that women are allowed to row in the Henley Royal Regatta, held in England each July.

13th **The FA's 10-year footballing ban** on Don Revie is overturned in the High Court.

18th **Mother Teresa** is awarded the Nobel Peace Prize.

20th **Council-house tenants** across the UK are invited to buy their homes under a new housing bill.

27th **Soviets storm Afghanistan:** the Kabul government falls as the Red Army brush aside opposition with a full-scale invasion by road and air. KGB assassins kill the Communist leader and family members. The Kremlin defends its actions saying the country asked for urgent help.

Charles Haughey

Afghanistan in turmoil after Soviet invasion

Index

COLLINS GEM
BABIES'
names
a nose of information

COLLINS GEM
BEER
a nose of information

COLLINS GEM
BIRDS
a nose of information

COLLINS GEM
CALORIE
Counter
a nose of information

COLLINS GEM
FACT FILE
a nose of information

COLLINS GEM
FENG SHUI
a nose of information

COLLINS GEM
FLAGS
a nose of information

COLLINS GEM
Healthy
EATING
a nose of information

COLLINS GEM
QUOTATIONS
a nose of information

COLLINS GEM
SAS
Self-Defence
a nose of information

COLLINS GEM
SAS
Survival Guide
a nose of information

COLLINS GEM
SEASHORE
a nose of information

COLLINS GEM
TREES
a nose of information

COLLINS GEM
Understanding
DREAMS
a nose of information

COLLINS GEM
WILD
flowers
a nose of information

COLLINS GEM
WINE
Dictionary
a nose of information